Visions of Reality
Illusions of Truth

Michèle Vachon Beaudin

Tallahassee, Florida USA

(c)2011 immi'ges & words press
All rights reserved

Prints can be purchased separately by contacting
us for pricing and details.

All original works of art in this publication are the
sole property of the author.

Book And Cover Design by Michèle Vachon Beaudin

www.immiges.com
www.immigesandwords.com

michele@immiges.com

ISBN 978-0-9826877-1-0

Library of Congress Control Number: 2010917053

Printed in the United States of America

First Edition

Nuit Sans Frontières

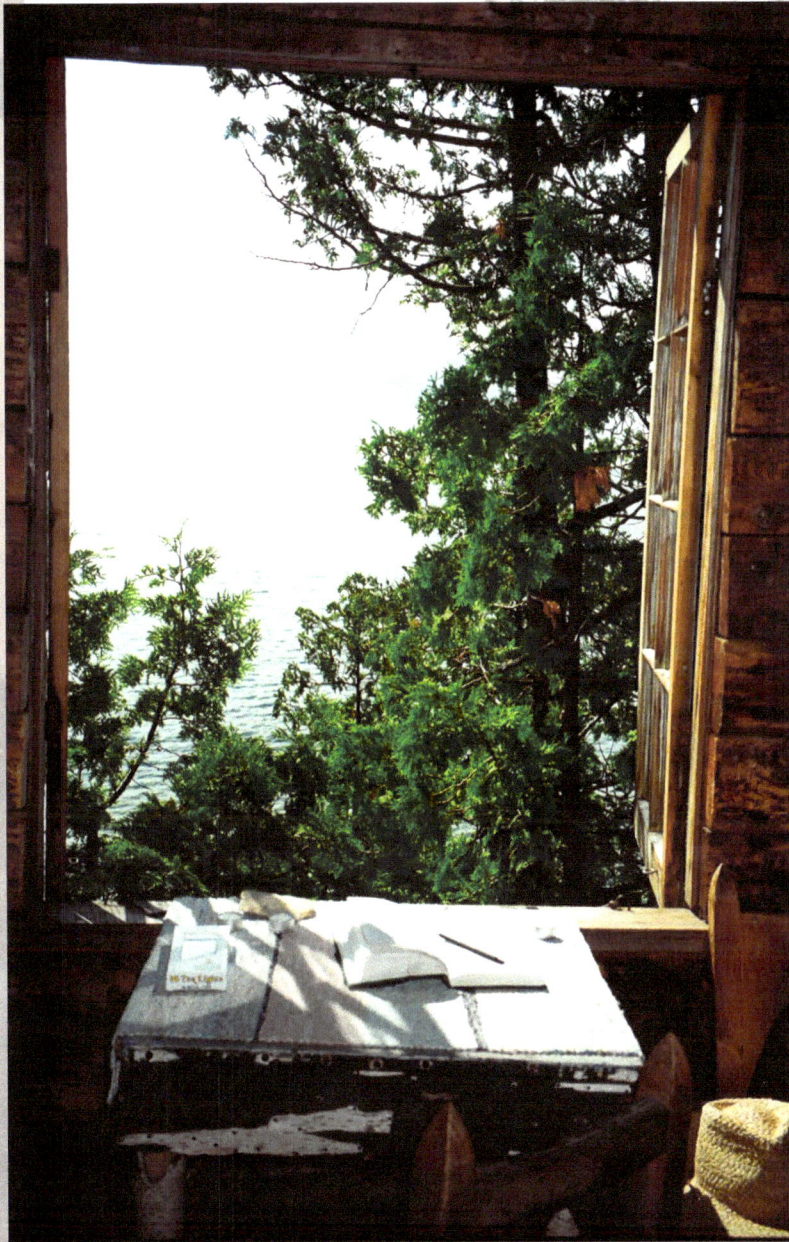

Just as there are no words
for the symphony of water
gently reaching the shore,
this haven of peace and solitude
that is the Cliff House
can only be lived
and not be spoken of with accuracy.

But we keep trying.

4:30 PM

The sun, seeping through
the window panes.
Cedar trees rising to meet the sky.
Sailboats gliding on the water.

A seagull wings by in a hurry,
she finds a mate,
they begin the dance of life.

A puff of clouds leaves a shadow
on the Bay.
A motorboat.
The charm is broken.

I am alone again.

4:45 PM Meditation

'A window opened to eternity.'

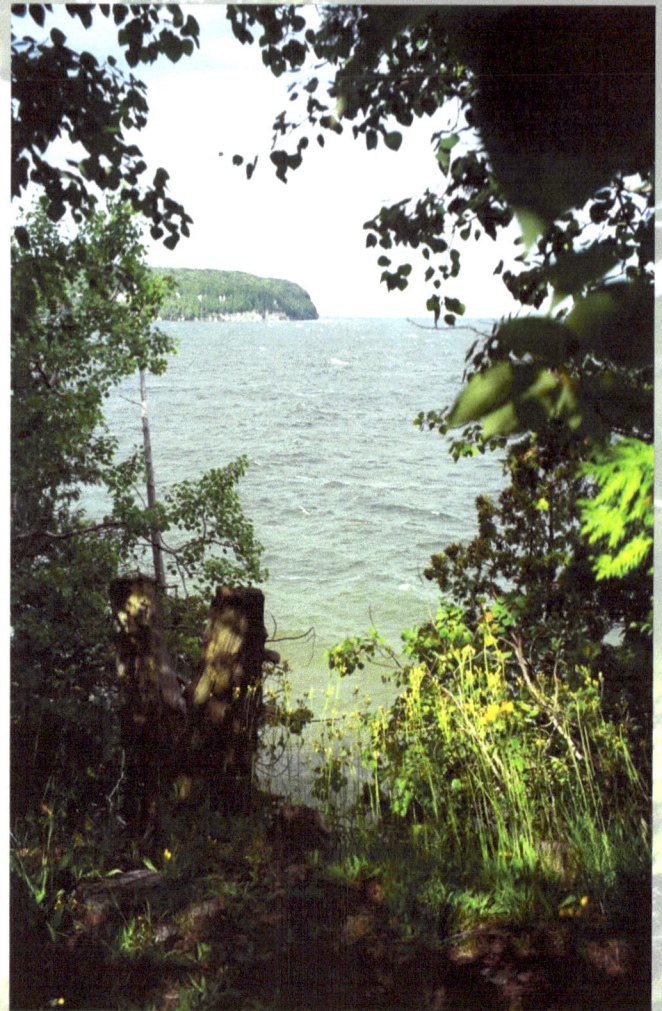

It once was called doing nothing.
Times change,
those we called lazy
are now philosophers.

Soon perhaps,
they will rule the world,
all in the name of
Meditation.

6:00 PM

There is a naked 'Y' at the top of the tree.
Is it talking to me, questioning my presence?
Or did an owl decide to carve
a slingshot to shoot the moon?

Is it a sickle?
If so, where is the hammer?
Is the cedar playing a joke,
pointing North, trying to trick the wind,
or hoping to confuse a hiker lost on a trail?

How did it happen?
Did the needles fall out?

But the main question is:

'Y'

The water goes north
but not in my window where it is eastbound.

What will happen if the currents finally meet?
Will the water rise up or fall down?

Flies, or perhaps mosquitoes,
are buzzing around my head
like so many helicopters
looking for a landing site.

6:45 PM

Outside the cabin, the air is still.
Only a faint rippling sound
tells me the water
is still coming up to lick the rocky shore.

Sunset.

Every minute counts.
The joining of sky and earth takes time.
The joining takes patience.

This nightly ritual,
everyday a different one,
today I can celebrate with my soul.

'Sky, water and earth,
today, the same as forever.'

7:45 PM

The sun wants to hide behind
the tallest of the cedars as though too
shy to set in my presence.

Scented candles, fragrant trees.

The seagulls are now silently wanting for
their world to end.

Some occasionally break the silence.

Did they forget the time?

8:15 PM

The blinding light has turned yellow.
Merger is eminent.
A dark line of the horizon takes my
illusions of forever away.

There is land where water was.

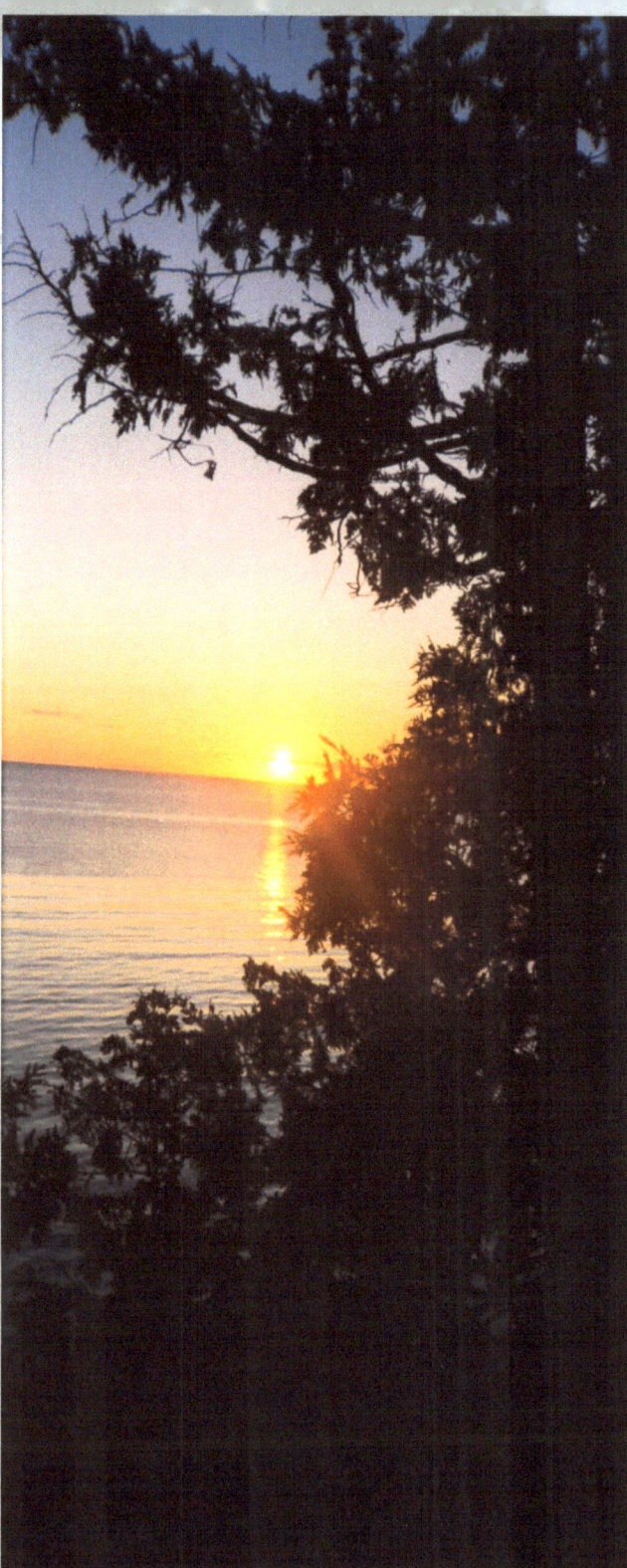

The sun is crashing,
turning this Midwestern shore
into a burning crater.

Thin cloud sharks swim around the site,
waiting to pick up the pieces,
perhaps dreaming of putting out the fire.

I sit here waiting.
Now above, now below, the cedar branches
serve as stepping-stones for the
descending sun.

Not yet orange, perhaps peach,
a giant circle still projects light
underlined by a procession of clouds.

The perfect stage for a perfect finale.

'We're all born for a reason.
I was born for today so I may live through
this night'

8:30 PM

My heart is now pounding, anticipating the final act.
Seagulls are now shadows, silent, waiting.

Red flames everywhere.
The water sizzles, crashing into these soundless fireworks,
now ready to end.

Like a watercolor splash, rays stretch in all directions.

I was wrong.
It isn't over:
The sun isn't collapsing,
it is ready to explode.

8:40 PM

The red is winning with the orange melting into its own light.
I am waiting.
The air is cooler, seemingly rising from the earth.
Night air.
The hour between dog and wolf.

The end of a perfect day,
the beginning of a perfect night.

The gulls go into a last frenzy,
the waves rise up and crash on the limestone,
then it is done.

Would life be worth living without
Wine for life,
Eyes to see,
and a pen and paper to share it all with the world?

The fire is roaring.
Literally.

Moths seek refuge in its flames.
The candles are burning.
I write in the glow of their fire.

The bay has turned into a dark meadow with swarms of birds hovering over it…
Or are those tiny ripples giving the illusion of life?

A single cloud hovers around, like a UFO searching for a prey.
First star… or maybe Venus.
I make a wish to live on forever.

The Black Box

There is a black box on the wooden chest.
It looks hostile, dark metal threatening.

It was once familiar, a friend almost.

Now I can't recall why.
My stories are hidden in its memory for all to find.
But are they?
Maybe they are still in my head, unable to escape the labyrinth of my mind.

I want the box to go away.
It scares me.

9:30 PM

The perfect branch.

just spotted the perfect branch,
long curving up to the sky,
spreading its toes for spiders
to nest and weave their webs.

It is the perfect branch.

But, no,
there is another perfect branch
right below it.

And another again under that one too!
My God, they are all perfect branches.

The night air crawls up the cliff and through my window.

I never believed in the night air,
but now I see its prints on my arms and hear it chatter up the cabin walls.

The window wants to close… I won't let it.

My back is hot from the fire; my ears are tuned to the voices of time.
I breathe-in life rising from the land.

Like an ivory almond
shelled for the occasion,
the moon turns its slivered face
towards the star…

Or is it Venus?

The window frame,
like a cosmic ladder,
reaches out to the sky,
ignoring the moon,
and loses its way
in the dark space of time.

I can always see the whole moon.

Can't everyone?

Staring at the fire,
I find it backwards.
I'd have to meld with the rocks
to see the images escaping from the logs.

The moon, like the broken face of a clock,
lopsided, slips into the dark sky,
defying the stars as it sinks to the ground
and marks the passage of time.

The night is getting darker, the lamp casts a deeper shadow,
the candles glow brighter.

Ghosts of tall trees now stand guard at the door.
I would never know the bay, save for the water sounds
that tell me of its presence.

10:00 PM

The fire is creeping around the log,
blues and purples caressing the charred wood.
The deep ambers whistle a tune
to accompany the sensuous dance.

There is still a hint of light on the horizon,
just enough to remind me
that tomorrow is the longest day.

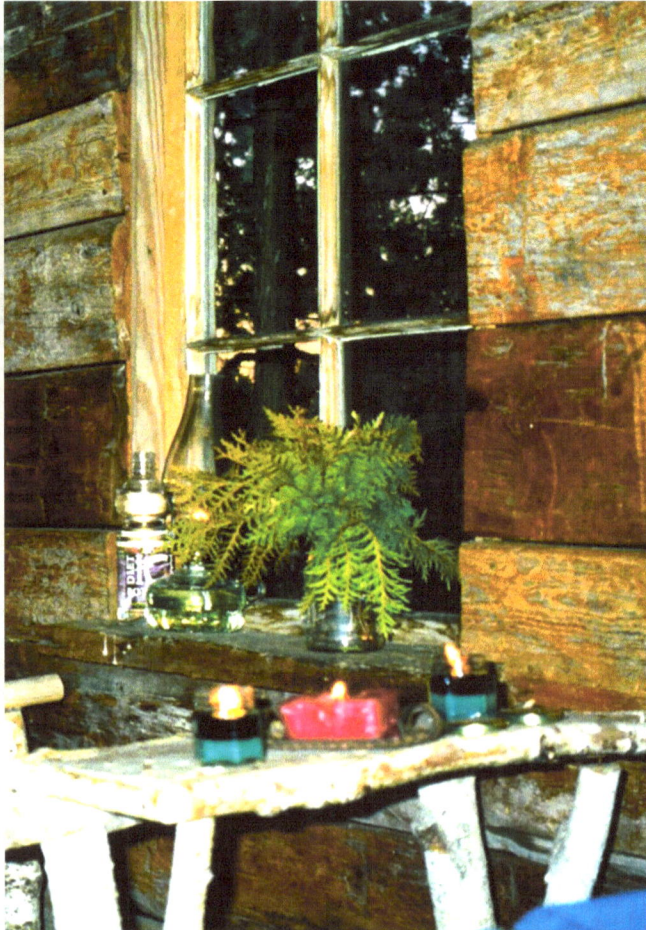

I wish I could save the scents
that fill the cabin
as I am capturing its images.

Only my memory
can store the sweet air
and awaken my senses
if I ever see that scent again.

All I need is one corner of life
to Live, love and die.'

There are twelve boards on the ceiling,
four beams to support them,
the floor is carved in limestone
the walls are made of logs.

My fire is burning into the cliff,
warming the walls around it.

How many tears were shed in this cabin?
How many hearts were broken or mended?
How many dreams were shattered or rekindled?
The answers are between these narrow walls.

Did anyone count the days left to live?
Did anyone find a reason to go home?
Why can't the wall tell me?
I have to know.
I need to know.
My soul is now one with these others.
What is this leading to? Where is this going?

10:15 PM

The fire is backwards again,
a reminder of life's whimsical spirit.

People called me brave for wanting this solitude.
Could anyone be scared in this sanctuary?

The peace,
the lulling sounds of water now crashing on the rocks
comfort and calm.
But still there can't be sleep
lest I miss even one moment in this timeless shelter.

I walk outside in order not to see the path.
I am rewarded by total darkness.
There is no time.
There is no space.
Just this cabin hanging onto a cliff,
trying to hold its breath until morning
when time and space return.

My original log is still burning.
I'm impressed:
I built the perfect fire…
Though backwards.

10:30 PM

The star… or Venus has marched across the window,
moon in tow, beaming as it goes.
Another star, a pale one this time,
follows in the moon's shadow,
yearning to join the hunt.

10:45 PM

There are elves moving in the fire,
tiny feet disturb the sizzling coal.
I sense their shadows dancing behind the logs.
But I only see them when I'm not looking.

Now reaching its climax,
the diminutive moon
lights up the entire bay.

A carpet of silver
or a pewter blue rug
covers what was water.

The moon pauses for effect
and my star… or Venus,
now wins the race,
gliding over the peninsula,
soon to cross the Canadian border.

Does the moon have a passport?

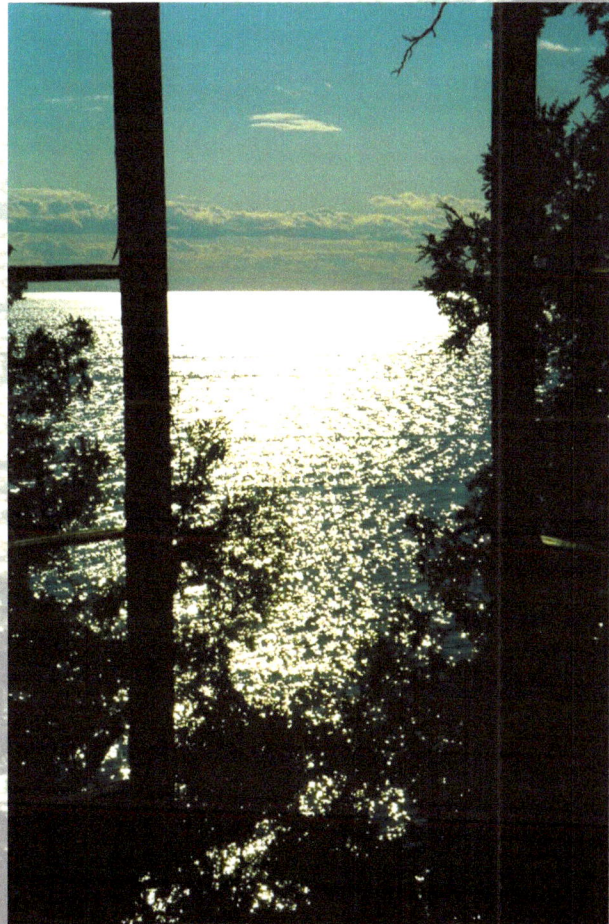

11:00 PM

My eyes go from the window to the log walls,
to the fire, the lamp,
then to the candles.

It's all so familiar.
My soul already knew of this refuge.

The hook holding the window in place falls back,
the window opens out to the night.

Why, How?

I have been here before.
In another time,
in a life I have lost.

I have existed in this space before.

I am reuniting with a long lost friend
and that friend is me.

Memories

I lived in a cliff house before.
How come I never noticed?

Was it a child's wedding?
Or another child's birth?

Too many losses?
Too much loneliness?

How could I not notice?

The path to the beach was steep.
The sunsets, unforgettable.

The third day of the full moon, the glowworms would mate:
Perched on a rock, a good view of the moonlit sea,
I watched the fireworks of minute lives eager to reproduce.

A sight worth waiting all month for.

My cliff house had beauty,
but my cliff house was a refuge from pain.

How come I never noticed I lived in a cliff house?

11:30 PM

Sleep.

It takes you away
to meet yourself in a land
where dreams want to escape.

I never want sleep, but sleep always wants me.

The candles are nearing death,
but the fire still burns.

I suspect its flames will glow through the summer
into fall and winter.

The next day
Summer's first steps.

5:00 AM

Another perfect day is born.
The gulls are waving at me from the shore.

There are no blemishes in the sky.

But, is it where lies the day's perfection?
No, it is perfect
Because it just is.

The tree with perfect branches
is there with its 'Y" at the top.
The clamor of water
which kept me secure in knowing I was alive
through the night…

Still there.

I also have faith,
although I can't see it,
that the sun will soon raise its head behind me
over the cliff.

One lonely log still simmers in the hearth.
One candle forgot to stop its vigil.

This moment will soon become history,
with last night as one of its best chapters.

5:45 AM

The light of day reminds me of what the black box is for:
A writing tool I usually cherish to use.

I carefully put it away, a precious cargo.

The only writing instrument that always takes my mistakes away.
Instantly, without prejudice,
without judging,
forever.

7:00 AM

The bell is calling. Today has begun.

Tomorrow is but a word.

On a meditative walk,

I happened upon a carpet of gold

and came face to face with with nature's wild side.

It brought a smile when none was before.

As I close this chapter,

my heart fills with a sense of longing,

a wish to one day recapture the essence of life

as I found it that night.

Michèle Beaudin was born in Montréal, Canada, later moved to the United States and now resides in Tallahassee, Florida, often retreating to her mountain cabin in Mentone, Alabama. While pursuing a career in international business and technology, she freelanced as a journalist for various newspapers and magazines. Her recent experience in Africa, as part of the Peace Corps served as an inspiration for her to dedicate her life creating and sharing beauty as a professional artist and author. Her award-winning photography and extensive collection of published articles, chap books and novels have a presence in four continent

By the same author:

Seasons On Lookout Mountain   ISBN 978-0-615-32453-1

With stunning images and beautiful prose, the author unveils the incredible beauty and serenity of Lookout Mountain throughout the seasons.

The Mountain   ISBN 978-0-615-33963-4

The author captures the unique beauty and spirituality of Scaly Mountain, North Carolina, with her original photographs accompanied by the prose the images inspired.

Novels:

Crossing the 50 Yard Line   ISBN 978-0-615-17157-9

Seven women, seven different stories. Three hundred and fifty years of life between them, but all feeling too young to give up or give in.

Crossing the Dream Line   ISBN 978-0-9826877-0-3

(2011 Living Book Awards Winner)
Ten years have passed since Barbara, Betsy, Clara, Jackie, Julie, Lucy and Patricia celebrated their 50th birthdays. As the women approach a new decade, they come face to face with dreams that may never come true and ones yet to be unleashed in their mind's eye.

These titles are available at all major on-line book stores or can be ordered from www.immigesandwords.com.

Looking through the window of Mertha's Cabin,
Let your own dreams lead your pen...

_____

_____

_____

_____

_____

_____

_____

_____

_____

_____

_____

_____

www.ingramcontent.com/pod-product-compliance
Lightning Source LLC
Chambersburg PA
CBHW060806090426
42736CB00002B/181